Additional praise for *This Bony Cabinet*

Inspired and unsettling, the images in *This Bony Cabinet*—be they personal or historic, political or religious, artistic or every day, born of the natural world or man-made super structures—remain long after the echoing refrain of life-death, life-death, and all that lies between first breath and last exhalation. Full of the exceptional and unexpected, revealing culture clashes, natural disasters, human terror, and intense individual observation, the poems challenge, both intellectually and emotionally, our ability to comprehend the awful ticking of the clock towards an inevitable—and often unprecedented—end. Here abides not only the power of story, but magical imaginings, brilliance, a fine meeting of sound created by odd words and poignant phrasing that stabs with clarity, then soothes with tender acceptance. What an impressive learning experience Kim Horner McCoy grants the reader—an opportunity to peek into people, places and events that are chock full of forgotten fragments, fragile skeleton secrets, and memorable resilience.
 —**Laurie Wagner Buyer**, author of *Across the High Divide* and *Reluctant Traveler*

This book cannot be a casual read. It challenges feelings of indifference and provokes an obligation from the reader to stop, examine, feel, and reflect. I truly enjoyed this book, even though I was convicted through most of it.
 —**Linda Apple**, author of *Write Life* and *Women of Washington Avenue*

Archaeological, forensic, and richly contemplative, these poems position McCoy as witness and interlocutor of calamity. "As with all questions," she writes, "destruction is a matter of point of view." Directing her gaze through the framing of art, photography, and history, McCoy attests to both the insufficiency and the prisming possibilities inherent in the work of any chronicler who attempts to fix a subject within a lens. In examples from science, history, architectural photography, journalism, and personal life, McCoy highlights how the edge of any frame implies the intentions of the framer and calls attention to what has been implied or left out. It is there, in the negative space, that McCoy creates a new vantage on her subjects. She paints objects with the shadows they cast and traces the impact of events through their aftermath. These poems sift through detritus, the "scrap and gristle" of gravesites, broken buildings, and storm paths littered with canceled checks and paper pulping in a field. The remnants evoke stories and suggest the fragmentary fragility of our lives. They imply the terrifying scale of events, a leviathan glimpsed by its bones. While these poems invite new perspectives on loss, tragedy, calamity (storms, suicide, accidents experienced and averted), their effect is not elegiac, but epistemological. In striking observations such as the "sun load" of the World Trade Center or the reflective capacity of the color blue in the sky that we remember framing it during the 9/11 attack, McCoy leads the reader to investigate what and how we know. The compassion with which she observes these fragments dissolves the margins between individual and collective suffering, highlighting how our pain calls to other pain, how "we are each other's disasters." These are sharp shards, meditatively sifted and reconfigured into a chandelier of eerily lovely, refracting glass. These poems are wise, thoughtful, simmering and shimmering.
 —**Amy Sage Webb-Baza**, author of *Save Your Own Life*

This Bony Cabinet is a title suggestive of the fragility voiced by the poems within it. These pieces deal delicately with the architectures of place, loss, and the walks we take toward meaning. Whether grounding us in the metal and beams of Chicago or the "flinty earth of Kansas," Kim Horner McCoy's poems work like tightly crafted prose, building their stories from weather, history, and found objects—as all my favorite poems do.
 —**Joey Brown**, author of *Oklahomaography* and *The Feral Love Poems*

This Bony Cabinet

poems by

Kim Horner McCoy

Finishing Line Press
Georgetown, Kentucky

This Bony Cabinet

Copyright © 2021 by Kim Horner McCoy
ISBN 978-1-64662-565-9 First Edition
All rights reserved under International and Pan-American Copyright Conventions. No part of this book may be reproduced in any manner whatsoever without written permission from the publisher, except in the case of brief quotations embodied in critical articles and reviews.

ACKNOWLEDGMENTS

The following poems appeared in slightly different form in these publications:

"Apocalypse," *Flint Hills Review* (Fall 2009)
"Flutter," *Little Balkans Review* 6.1.78 (Spring 2011)
"The Rookery, La Salle Street, Chicago," *Potpourri* 11.4. 66 (1999)

Publisher: Leah Huete de Maines
Editor: Christen Kincaid
Cover Art: Luke Carter
Author Photo: Luke Carter
Cover Design: Elizabeth Maines McCleavy

Order online: www.finishinglinepress.com
also available on amazon.com

Author inquiries and mail orders:
Finishing Line Press
PO Box 1626
Georgetown, Kentucky 40324
USA

Table of Contents

OF THE FORUM

The Rookery, LaSalle Street, Chicago 1
The Salvage Artist 2
Flutter 5
At the Grave of Billy the Kid 7
For Which it Stands 8
Fugitive 10
Windows on the World 11

IN, OF, FROM THE OUTSIDE

Infinity 13
Orienteering 14
Apocalypse 16
First Supper 17
Walking Along 18
Introducing 21
Black Swan White 22

THROUGH THE DOOR

Forensis 23
Guarding Pollock 26
Drumbeat 28
Premise 29
{The Empty Set) 30
Streetlight at Sunrise 32
Geese at Midnight 33

Forensis: adj, L. Of the forum. In, of, from the outside. Through the door.

Origins: A Short Etymological Dictionary of Modern English. (1958) by Eric Partridge

OF THE FORUM

The Rookery, LaSalle Street, Chicago

All that's left of their black path is paralyzed
    Flight, their dance in relief,

Their raucous calls abstracted into masonry and brass
    (A fine twist as they are known thieves

And mimics, liable to carry off small shiny
    Things—pocket watches, ladies' rings,

Voices of the newly dead), and the spiral
    Stair, convolution tightening

From eye-shot to invisibility, from the wide
    Inside aim to an imaginary

Point, sharp as reflex. Feel yourself like smoke rising,
    Disorganizing just before you meet

Nickel's stare, his next-to-never vision. Before his wild
    Flash fixes your assent,

Dive a little, swoop, cry out, before his camera crucifies
    You, clinging to the thinning center.

Richard Nickel (1928-1972): architectural photographer, whose photos of The Rookery were instrumental in saving it from the wrecking ball.

The Salvage Artist

1.   Ornament

Sullivan's lobed leaves
                clutch at buildings,
consummate oak (whose leaves refuse to fall).

Nickel photographed it broken:
                a concrete tendril propped on his car,
                mosaic vines between wreckers' hands,
                the sky in a demolished wall.

You may call this manufactured,
                this assemblage of fact and fragment into my own images,

this dressing of faulty imagination with Sullivan's baroque
ornament and Nickel's granite obsession.

2.   Reconstruction

They dumped much of Nickel's ornament into the lake
and the debris from the Fire became the land
on which the Art Institute stands.

Except. An arcade
from the Garrick decorates the entrance to Second City,
and before they wrecked the Stock Exchange,
they pieced out Sullivan's Trading Room, reassembled it—
a whole room,
enshrined as Art.

Was Sullivan baroque? His revelation
came in the Sistine.
                For two days, he sat crook-necked and gazing

at that ceiling, reveled in Michelangelo's muted blues, buried golds,
his varnished skins, found the Superman

he had long desired, and his faith erupted
into clotted Thoreauvian prose,
into ornamentation that declared
                              a building's place in nature.

3.   Self-Portraits

of Richard Nickel temporize.
He meets his own camera as though on a dare,
as though pugnacity
were a virtue.

He's about to shower off the grime of his scavenging,
or he captains a tall building,
or he's so far inside an empty room it's impossible to see
his features.

Nickel aimed for documentary:
                              he'd learned salvation was denied
to buildings, so he stripped facades,
claimed ornament,
pictured himself on scaffolding.

He knew that "I or any other photographer creeps in no matter
how hard he tries not to."

4.   Audience

Roadside crosses, painted white and staked into the right-of-way,
punch blunt apertures into the sky, decorate

equally interstates and backroads.
Trimmed in polyester ribbon and plastic foliage, lettered in
                                        weatherproof black,

they demand our sympathy for the unknowns
who bought it when they crossed the center line. With their arrogant

uprights and transverse conceits, they mock our mating, command
our attention for the ones who left their beloveds with nothing

but anonymous crosses.
Crusades usually end with someone losing something.

I lost you. Sullivan lost wife, friends, reputation. Chicago lost
the ornament

but Nickel was found, in his biographer's words,
"crushed and twisted between two I-beams,

one of which had fallen across his shoulder
blades, and a longer one that had fallen

lengthwise across the lower part of his body,"
in the wreckage of the Exchange.

See Richard Cahan's They All Fall Down *and Louis Sullivan's*
Autobiography of an Idea.

Flutter

The day the Fokker died,
and the Kansas sky
dropped alike passengers

and pilot onto the flinty
Kansas earth, the Rock
was famous for his winning

record, for his Gipper
speech, for lifting the game
from the turf to the air.

I suppose the pilot (a man
named Fry, though
you'd never know it if all

you'd read was the plaque
in the I-35 McDonald's)
knew the weight

of the fame he ferried.
He must have been worried
about the weather,

the low ceiling, the cold,
whether the rain
had loosened the glued joints.

In the end, it was flutter
(motion, NASA says "that is akin
to shimmy" in a car)

that did them in
that snapped the wing
spar, splintering

the wood of rib and skin.
If you know it's there,
the memorial stone points

skyward from the ridge,
visible through binoculars,
faintly gray behind a screen

of winter trees. A gravel
road spirals up the hill,
dead-ending at the Heathman

place (home of the boy
named Easter, among the first
to reach the wreck).

And if, having hit that country
cul-de-sac, and turned back,
and outrun the barking dogs,

you stop midway, and cut
your engine, and step
from your car, you'll see

not the least flutter
of leaf or feather, hear neither
wind nor song.

At the Grave of Billy the Kid

The water left a deposit of reddish clay and fine sand where it was sluggish, and coarse sand where it was swift . . .
        Destructive Floods in the United States 1904, USGS

As with all questions, destruction
is a matter
of point of view. Your tiny cairn
looks to you
like Art but your collecting wrecked
somebody's habitat.

The grave may be a fine and private
place but what
if Billy isn't in it anymore?
What if he'd
barely turned to bones before
the Pecos

jumped its banks and washed him
clean away?
What possesses tourists, pilgrims, poets
to reach
between the bars encaging both his head
and foot stones

deposit pebbles, pennies, bullets,
not to mention
the oyster shell suspended from a cord of braided hemp
swinging like a key?
Three hours south, snake and scorpion and paw
prints

speak of prey or poison or power but I
can make
nothing of the lines arranged in mazes
or the quartered
spheres encircled by seventeen, by twenty-three
spots.

For Which it Stands

6,400: American flags sold by Wal-Mart on Sept. 11, 2000.
116,000: American flags sold by Wal-Mart on Sept. 11, 2001.
    "The Numbers" TIME Magazine

Hauled out of closets and attics,
untangled

from the remnants of Independence
Days,

unfurled
like umbrellas

at the first clap of thunder.
They began flapping

from plastic poles
clipped to car roofs and fenders:

One man mounted
a full-sized Glory,

its banner the length of his flat bed,
drove it up and down

the streets
as though he marshalled a parade.

Overnight,
lawns sprouted vinyl

signs, stripes printed so as to fake
the billow and wave, campaign for solidarity.

At every checkout,
tiny Glories bloomed.

Bunting crawled
across every television spot.

Shop window dummies
sported bicentennial bell-bottoms,

and mannequins modeled
star-spangled teddies.

The body
of the flag is called the "fly,"

the star-shot blue field
is the "union,"

and according to United States Code,
Title 4, Chapter 1,

the flag
is a living thing.

Better we should have veiled
our faces, cut our hair,

draped every mirror in black crepe.

Fugitive

Memory insists on blue skies
that morning. As though that made it worse.
As though with a proper red warning
we could have braced for the waves

that rippled not just through the Towers down
to bedrock, but west through every time
zone and telecast. As though red would have paused
our gazing at the last five seconds those bodies
falling against the televised sky ever knew.

But the sky when you're in it
isn't blue, any more than water is when you
squat and scoop. The first time I flew, sitting in the blue
upholstered seat, I imagined walking

on the clouds. I expect sailors know
the same thing pilots do: that blue makes no promise,
that gravity has no color. *Fugitive* is the word
painters use for the way blue fades,
the way white takes over, over time.

Windows on the World

We are all guilty. Voyeurs after the fact, we orient
ourselves to the far distant act. Pearl Harbor
exploded six months before my mother arrived.
JFK died while I lay swaddled, mute, unknowing.

On that blue September morning, my daughter's principal
strode from room to room, stopping all the TVs
until every teacher started them again.
I remember Vietnam, Watergate, the hostages

from clips, quick cuts, commercials.
Likewise Waco, Oklahoma City: blooming smoke,
taped flames the same peculiar orange. This time
we watched for days, the dreadful loops

crashing and collapsing, knowing,
every single time,
                how it ended. People trapped inside
the Towers that morning phoned out
to friends or family: "Turn on the TV, tell me

what's happening." We called the spot Ground Zero
and before the dust of pulverized concrete and vaporized human beings
settled, the Tower's remaining steel beams
were sliced up, shipped to foundries around the world,

recycled into refrigerators, rebar, parts for all the cars
we've driven since. We are, each of us, the bearers
of our own and each other's disasters,
hemmed in by our skins, by our failures to convey

the fullness of either our misery or our ecstasy.
Sex is the antidote, we hope, the embodied metaphor,
the witness borne,
solution not just to pain and fear and loss, but to the singularity
each of us carries,
                the solitary fault each of us secretly knows

we own, the line along which we'll fall
apart. Architects speak of the sun load a building bears,
heat flashing red from the narrowest window,
beating against the glazing we imagine

will save us. Impact did not bring the Towers down.
The pinstripe beams acted as they were meant to act:
formed arches over the gaping holes the hijacked
jet planes punched, redistributed

gravity's load to the whole remaining members. But not even steel
can long withstand flame. Once, we thought the eye carried
light outward, cast a beam creating the thing
upon which the gaze fell, believed fire lived in the eye.

Now we know
                it's objects that return the light, bearing
not the red the sky possesses, but the blue it rejects.
Now we know
                we soak up images, turn them into dreams
of falling, fleeing, flying, Jungian horror stories

in which the monsters really do eat us. Aristotle taught us tragedy,
its nature as the fall of giants, our need to see the hero crash
and burn and rise again, defeat the villain
and get the girl before we turn the TV off and go to bed

where we're left, each of us, lonely as Atlas, sentenced
to hold up—arms trembling, legs shaking,
breath panting, heart pounding—
not only each other, not only the puny, spinning earth,

but, night after night, the terrible weight of the heavens,
the burden of our own ill-starred sky.

Windows on the World (1976-2001) was a restaurant on the top floor of the North Tower of the original World Trade Center.

IN, OF, FROM THE OUTSIDE

Infinity

Because it began
in sympathy.

Because it was the sun not death that stretched the rattlesnake
across the rocky trail soaking in October,
his skin the same pale as the dust,
puzzled in umber and mud and snuff.

Because it was the eye-stripe that mimicked
the flickering bluestem
and the bison over the ridge,
their absent hooves
deep and definite
as the shovel my mother

used to swing at every innocent
garter- grass- blacksnake
minding its business in the lespedeza,
Genesis and the maybe fang
outlawing empathy.

Because he buzzed,
sudden, twined himself into the symbol.

Because he stopped
me, one strike away, and stayed an eight
on his half of the path as I walked on
fear in one hand, yes in the other.

Orienteering

No one could have tracked
the action of that path,
a story I said

would help us back. I lied
of course, my shuffled
trail through ankle high leaves

lasted no longer than bread
crumbs scattered or pebbles dropped
by fairy tale children abandoned,

which we were not.
Still, I wanted the forest. In April,
dogwoods foam and redbuds

moan, hickory and oak explode
pollen, flowers, leaves
unbounded. A wall, solid

seeming, an arcade—
the space of a bow shot—and
we're off—horsemen, hart, hounds—

Stop.
These are not those woods.
It was November. Branches bare,

sky clouded,
the floor a history deeper than desire,
every trunk identical

—except for those alleged mosses—
to my eye. Headings, bearings,
navigation, matter to leaves

as much as I did. Matter to leaves.
Indeed,
that is the first direction, but the second

undoes the first and we're back
to my shuffled path,
my feet crunching.

Apocalypse

Yesterday, from among the new crop
                              of rocks,
I picked up half a harness buckle,
                          crusty with rust,

a crazed wedge of dinner plate, clay stained
and faintly flowered about the rim,

and two blue shards of glass, their edges
        ground smooth against stone.

Today, I found the head of a farrier's hammer,
pitted and dull, a harrow short three teeth,

and the snapped off blade of a hunting knife,
with, some inches away, its softly rotting handle.

These are the remains
                this earth gives up after days of rain:

the bones of farming, broken and boiling
                      up through the red mud.

Here, the end won't be volcanic,
                the earth won't belch flame

and spew fire and breathe ash. Instead
she'll quietly contract,
                pushing to the surface all
her scrap and gristle for us to sort through.

First Supper

The touch of a tongue
uncurling
          Cold probe
licking the salt bead
rhymes
with nothing

If my hand were attached
to my dead
body
stretched out in the middle of this copse
          draped across this rock—

swirl of cooling
fingers
palm
wrist—
the kiss
of this single
          Hoary comma

would be the beginning
of a congregation
a fluttering puddle of tongues and color

But today
only
this one invisible mouth
sucking on my skin
taking eating this
is my body
flying

Walking Along

Coyote was walking along
that's how the stories begin
and I know
I haven't any right
I'm too white to invoke Coyote
but it's the rhythm

Coyote was going along

and
not looking out
not looking both ways
mostly only
looking back inside behind his own eyes
always a mistake
because then the nowhere opens
and fuck

out comes

Twister
Cancer
Rattlesnake

and you can't fucking
believe it
walking along
because you cannot
love

Cancer / Rattlesnake / Twister

cannot love
        indifference
cannot believe
        irrelevance

Except

Cancer was skulking along
and if I'm too white for Coyote
for Cancer I'm too alive
nonetheless

Cancer was going along

and
not looking out
not looking both ways
mostly only
taking eating looking for things he could use
always wise
because then the nowhere opens
and

Phil

and we cannot fucking believe it

Then

Twister was blowing along
and if for Coyote I'm too white
and for Cancer too alive
for Twister I am definitely too whole
nonetheless

Twister was going along

and
not looking back
always looking only one way
definitely only
taking eating looking for things he could raze

always wise
because then the nowhere opens
and

Joplin

and I cannot fucking believe it

Finally

Rattlesnake was sliding along
and this is how the story ends
and I know
what you're thinking
but you're wrong
it *is* the rhythm

Rattlesnake was going along

and

not looking at all but taking
eating undulating
making a path
only as wide as his long body
always right
because then the nowhere opens
and

I

am walking along

Introducing

Each person has a clock measuring how long they have been buried on the island. You can stop their clock of anonymity and restore their history by adding a story to The Traveling Cloud Museum.
 —*The Hart Island Project website*

When does anonymity begin? In the womb
you don't know who you are, so why do we crave
a name at the limestone end? Suppose
you were buried with a mirror—not an iPhone
locked on selfie, but a frame of silvered
glass set in the lid like a pearl. Whom

do we imagine looking, whom do we want
to see standing at the back of the room
chanting our one, our only name? How many flames
do we need? At my worst, I used to fantasize
my unattended death, whether accident
or other, and wonder not who but when
>   or if my body would be recovered. You were
>   cremated and your ashes—I don't know. That clock

keeps ticking. And what about the leopard (so called
because its skin imitates the one big cats evolved)
slug I met on the sidewalk this morning, motion so slow
it looks like stillness, who carries its whole shell (so
like an oyster's) inside its spotted hide, a calcite shield
upon which ride the spirits of the rotting leaves it eats.

Orson Welles, H.G. Wells, Wells Fargo
George Orwell. Students refuse to choose
the difference and maybe they're right
to see the ghosted Georges as one more tack
I'm taking in the course of convincing them
that some people matter more than others.
>   As though we were not, each of us, cargo
>   and carrier both of that anonymous clock.

Black Swan White

Could we ever follow
fast enough to keep always
in the light? No one knows
everything but inside

every head some pain
must call, trumpeting
like to like, like magnets
drawing blood, like iron

filing every wrong done,
every slight imagined,
every white, gliding answer
inside this bony cabinet.

THROUGH THE DOOR

Forensis

1.
Nothing is permanent
except death, and even if that's so
there's no way to report it.

What remains are traces:

a boy five days lost in a pond,
handprints on humid cinder blocks,
the blood banked in my veins.

And nothing incorporates.
Especially not Jesus. At least, not the way they claimed.

What remains is evident:

X-rays and bank statements and grocery lists
pulping in a field hundreds of miles from here

homework and family photos (famously)
and cash and couch cushions and twisted

aluminum lawn chairs
teddy bears and syringes and handguns and dildos

and clothes—
a single pant leg with one pocket inside-out

a left sleeve hanging from its shoulder
all the lost buttons and belt buckles and laces

and so many odd running shoes, work-boots, flip-flops, stilettoes
trashed and scattered along the interstate.

You can count imaginary crosses
like faces in clouds or wallpaper streaked and soggy,
but they're still nothing

but mangled I-beams, accidents of physics
exactly like the red brick chimney
impaled by a white pine two-by-four

or the bicycle hanging
off the porch rail of a house the wind dis-integrated.

2.
Always there's the wind
in the image—

black gouts of smoke

leftover clouds

leaves and shingles and shreds
of everything.

3.
The wind *is* personal. A tornado is designated by the speed its wind attains, true enough, but also by how much it "eats," and yes, Dusty is a fictional character and so is Jo who knows the storm "comes after you," and, yes, the twisters they chase are digital but that does not render the words any less true.

It. Comes. After. You.

It shrouds
itself in rain
because it knows its job
and dresses so.

Guarding Pollock

You painted on the floor,
attacking the canvas
from every side, winding olive into white, spinning slate over taupe.

You slung paint the way the cowboy you claimed to be
would have thrown a rope.

Slashed crimson, spun rose, skeined
cream and green and yellow
                                     veiled
                                     laced
                                     crocheted

because damned if any of your bulls

or horses or hurt showed through. Except,
there is *1A* into which you pressed

                                     serial black prints

of your own hand. Were you thinking of Chauvet?
Your barn a cave, the sun your personal torch?

But here *One* is properly hung,
and the guard in his tidy blue suit motions
                                     me out of reach.

He does not actually grasp my wrist,
merely shakes his head, waves me back,
                                     forces me

to stand behind the sparkle tape
masking the floor,
                        like the mica edging

the stairs in my building,
(sand, grit, cinders, cigarette butts)

to keep me from slipping, pitching
handfirst into you.

Drumbeat

> ... *the Science and Security Board today moves the Doomsday Clock*
> *20 seconds closer to midnight—closer to apocalypse than ever.*
> Bulletin of the Atomic Scientists, January 23, 2020

Does it matter
     which disaster
the doomsday clock
threatens
to chime when
     the woodpecker
excavates
her home one
plockplockplock

at a time?
Those shreds
     of dead wood
she
relegates
to the wind matter

to sparrows and wrens and starlings and cardinals.
     Which direction
would save us?

       Away from sugar and gender and profit?
       Away from guns and greed and screens?
       Away from clatter and tribes and lies?

The door
she drilled
opens an echo
     into which
she disappears
and now
     that maple's sapped
branch
reverberates.

Premise

—supposing you brought the light inside the body—
       The President of the United States, 23 April 2020

Suppose we tipped our heads back,
veed our mouths like beaks, and grain
by grain the sun ticked in. Suppose
shining were solid, like smoke or pollen.

Suppose, like the ocean, the moon
broke, sucking the speech from under
our feet like spoons full of sugar. Suppose
glowing could gather, like a magnet

feathering iron. Suppose, like corn,
we could peel our troubles, reveal
each pearled packet, each sweetly
gleaming photon, each quantum seed.

Suppose I decided, for the moment,
to mimic the enemy, as catbirds do.

{The Empty Set}

If this were a crime
scene {library, office, tool shed}
in an antique mystery novel, the detective
would fill with plaster the treads I left. January
grass flattened and a beer bottle, brown
beneath a dormant pear tree three
months from its carrion
bloom.

The other cars
slotted into their tidy boxes.
Their proper blossoms guard no bier, no
coffin, no body. No pointed chin. No clenched grin.
Once, we talked all night long. Once, we had a standoff
over who would take the garbage out. {Riesling,
gingerbread men, The Rolling Stones} Years
I surrendered. Instead, the close-up
(pointed chin, clenched grin)
with which they filled
your place.

I will not
come at you slant. You
surrendered what you *would have*
wanted with that bullet. Once, we locked
ourselves out of the house. Once, we went looking
for the Spook Light {lantern, headlight, will o' the wisp}.
This morning, unthinking, I pulled on a pair of black and white
ragg socks you gave me once for Christmas. They were always
baggy. And they're cotton so they aren't even warm.
It was cold that night. You put your coat on.
You put your coat on. You put
your coat
on?

You are dead
fourteen days and overnight
fog froze onto tree limbs and power lines,
the slant of car windows, and the angles of Stop signs.
Crystals furring. No—that solution of bluing, alum, salt was long
before I knew you. And the rabbit jacket. {Red striped
dress, pink Oxford shirt, knit tie}
They were
us.

Streetlight at Sunrise

There are some rules. Dead people stay
dead. (Was that motivation?) Light circles
seven and a half worlds per second
(according to *Space*) but that's no help

to goodbye. (Nor is Superman who is now
speeding faster, speeding farther, turning
the earth back, not in the comics, nor in
the body of Christopher Reeve (1952-2004)

but in this poem because I could not stop
him.) Why a Carriage, reckon? Nowadays
there's often not even a hearse. Let alone
a body in it. Well, we haven't time

have we, for the pomp and the ceremony?
It holds up traffic and wrecks the worddday
and as for Dickinson's Swelling House
(1890, same year the census burned)

archeologists of the future will excavate
landfills. We have slide shows instead
of barrows. (As though we could turn people
into photons, choose between light and death.)

Maybe it's simple contrast, the way that streetlight
sparks against the rags of yesterday's storm,
the way I keep coming back to outrage, the way
your bullet baffles . . . everything. Not just sleep

and memory, but lectures and yoga and television
and tea. Because you (1962-2019) would not wait
for crocuses, or high tide, or chemistry, because
you could not narrow your way out of the dark.

Geese at Midnight

When toward the end of *Citizen Kane*
                        Susan Alexander understands
what time it is
doors
       slam against jambs against jambs against jambs.

Whereas in memory
                Remingtons and Royals and Smith

Coronas gallop ahead, tonight the *whapwhapwhap*
                        of the Life Flight banking
clatters the panes
        in their frames.

Always there's the shift
                of sirens and geese and attitude.
According to Partridge those things are *absurd*

which do not train in harmony.
When you cooked, pans crashed, cabinets
                            banged. That flat slap.

Feynman and Gell-Mann and Hawking claim Time
mirrors
       motion, but until we manage quantum hearts,

quarks do us about as much good as hammers
                          in a glass factory.

Kim Horner McCoy grew up in the Ozarks and lives now in the shadow of the Flint Hills. She admits to being a cat person, but is otherwise agnostic, and along with her husband has for years been threatening to turn their breakfast table conversation into a podcast. She has been a university adjunct instructor in Missouri and Kansas since 1996, has published poems, short fiction, and reviews in various journals, and is currently working on her first full-length collection of poems, *The Woman's Belief Corps*.

www.ingramcontent.com/pod-product-compliance
Lightning Source LLC
LaVergne TN
LVHW041558070426
835507LV00011B/1167